THE FIRST BOOK OF
THE
CALIFORNIA GOLD RUSH

by WALTER HAVIGHURST

pictures by HARVE STEIN

FRANKLIN WATTS, INC.
575 Lexington Avenue • New York 22

Contents

Gold on the American River

WHEN James Marshall woke in his cabin, he heard the familiar sound of water. He dressed and went outside. No one was stirring in the camp, and the winter sun had not yet climbed over the ridge of mountains. The only sound in this California wilderness was the rushing of snow-water in the American River. It was January 24, 1848.

Jim Marshall had traveled as far as a man could go in America. From New Jersey he had wandered west to the Ohio Valley. He was a good carpenter and he could get work wherever he stopped. In 1844 he joined a caravan of a hundred wagons bound for Oregon. Marshall had no wagon; he rode on horseback, carrying his sack of carpenter's tools. After wintering in Oregon, he went south to California.

At Sutter's Fort in the Sacramento Valley he took a job repairing wagons. John Sutter had come from Switzerland, hoping to make his fortune in America. Now he had a big tract of land farmed by Indians and Mexicans, and he was enlarging the trading post in his fort.

To provide building lumber for settlers, Jim Marshall proposed to build a sawmill in the mountains. He chose a site on the American River where there was a steady flow of water between richly timbered hills. The river would float the lumber down to Sutter's Fort. Marshall had a good location, and Sutter furnished men and supplies to build the mill. Marshall could not know that his mill-race, a trench that carried water to turn the mill wheel, would change the course of history.

In January, 1848, the mill was finished, but Marshall found that the wheel was set too low to turn freely. The millrace must be deepened. With pick and shovel, the men dug at the trench during the short winter days. At night they opened the wooden gate to let the water wash out loose rock and gravel.

On the morning of January 24, when no one else was stirring, Marshall shut off the water to see if the channel was washed clean. While he walked along the trench, the sun came over the mountains. The sky was blue and clear. It would be a fine day.

Marshall was a moody man, habitually silent. He had lived much alone, and if he had thoughts he kept them to himself. He usually wore a glum expression. But when he stopped at the side of the millrace, his eyes filled with interest. From the bottom of the ditch, under a few inches of water, something glinted. He scooped a hand in the cold water and brought up a bit of metal. It was heavier than gravel, and when the water drained away it shone with a dull yellow color. He laid it on a ledge and pounded it with a stone. The metal did not break, but it bent under the blow. It was malleable.

3

A few minutes later Marshall startled the men in the messroom with a beaming smile. "I think I've found a gold mine," he said.

The workmen were not interested. No one had ever found gold in California. The pellets in Marshall's hand were probably worthless. "Fool's gold" had deceived many men in the western mountains.

Jim Marshall was a stubborn man. He said no more about his discovery, but the next morning he walked slowly along the millrace, examining every crevice in the rocky bed. Then he walked along the river where the water swirled around rock ledges. Several times he picked up bits of the yellow metal and kept them. On the fifth day he tied his specimens in a handkerchief and climbed onto his horse. He told the men he was going down the valley to look for a supply wagon.

It was fifty miles from the mill to Sutter's Fort. That night Marshall slept under an oak tree beside the river. He was used to being alone, but he was not used to the thoughts that swirled in his mind. The river ran through miles of mountain canyon, washing at rock banks and ledges. If there was gold in the mountains, the river would bring it down. Heavier than sand, it would settle in bars and ledges. In the past few days he had collected a handful of specimens. Whatever it was, more was waiting to be found. At last the rushing river lulled him to sleep.

Daybreak came gray and heavy. He rode on down the valley in a drenching rain. His clothes were dripping when he walked into Sutter's office.

Sutter asked about the sawmill, but Marshall did not seem to hear him. He untied his handkerchief and spilled the yellow stuff onto the table. Sutter stared in silence. He turned a nugget in his fingers, rapped it on a board, scratched it with a knife blade.

"It's heavy," Marshall said, "and malleable."

Sutter weighed the nugget on a scale and tested it with acid. Now his eyes were as bright as Marshall's.

"It's gold," he said. "High-grade gold. Where did you find it?"

"In the millrace," Marshall said, "on the American River."

Marshall and Sutter had discovered gold. But they could not guess how far that word would travel, or how many adventurous and hopeful men it would draw to far-off California. Two weeks after their discovery, the United States signed a treaty with Mexico paying $15 million for a vast western territory between the Rocky Mountains and the Pacific. Within two years the California gold mines had yielded that amount three times over.

Sam Brannan's Secret

MARSHALL and Sutter agreed to keep their discovery secret; they did not want to start a stampede to the American River. Back at the sawmill the work went on as though nothing had happened. The men had forgotten Marshall's yellow flakes and pellets. They did not know the secret.

But they would soon find out.

On a Sunday morning a young Mormon mill hand named Henry Bigler took his gun from the bunkhouse to go hunting. When he was out of sight of the camp he put down his gun and began hunting — for gold. When he returned empty-handed, his friends taunted him for being a poor hunter. But in a buckskin bag in his pocket, Bigler had some yellow dust.

After that day Bigler became a determined hunter. Every Sunday he put his gun on his shoulder and went up or down the American River. On Washington's Birthday, when the rest of the men sat around the stove, he tramped off in a snowstorm. Nobody could hunt in such weather, but Bigler came back triumphant. From his buckskin pouch he spilled out $25 worth of gold. For these men that was a month's wages.

Now all the mill hands started prospecting. As soon as the day's work was done, they went digging into sandbars and picking at rock crevices with hunting knives. Some of them left the camp to look for gold farther up the valley.

When a teamster came to camp with a wagonload of supplies, one of the workmen gave him a nugget for a souvenir. On his return to Sutter's Fort, the teamster went to Sam Brannan's store. He asked for a bottle of brandy and threw down the gold to pay for it. With shrewd eyes Sam Brannan studied the nugget. After a few questions, he put the gold in his pocket. Then he seemed to forget it.

A few weeks later Sam Brannan went to San Francisco. The nugget was burning in his pocket, and a secret was burning in his mind. At last he could contain it no longer. Riding horseback through the San Francisco plaza, he waved his hat and shouted: "Gold! Gold! Gold from the American River!"

His words sent a frenzy through the town. Storekeepers closed their doors and headed for the Sierra Nevada Mountains. The schoolmaster left his schoolroom. Printers hurried out of the newspaper office. Soldiers walked off their posts. Sailors abandoned their ships in the harbor. Within a week, three-fourths of San Francisco's population had gone prospecting.

Soon gold began to arrive from diggings along the American River. More men left San Francisco, and the frenzy spread to other towns in the region. The old capital city of Monterey was left without soldiers or workmen. In the new town of Sonoma, two-thirds of the houses were empty. In San Jose, nine-tenths of the men hurried off for the gold mines.

These men were leaving homes, families, and business for a vision of shining gold in the mountains. Some piled food and blankets into wagons and creaked off toward the Sacramento. Others loaded horses with bulging packs. Many walked, carrying a blanket roll, a pick and shovel, and a washpan to dip up the gold-bearing sands.

This swarm of prospectors headed for Sutter's Fort, where the American River joined the Sacramento. Suddenly that lonely outpost became a crowded place, full of wild rumors and reports. At Mormon Island, men said, solid gold nuggets had been taken out of the river. At Coloma, where Jim Marshall had built his mill, the ground glinted with flakes of gold. At the falls of the river, men were spading up golden sand.

Now that Sutter's Fort was the most populous place in California, Sam Brannan had a rush of business. Outside his trading post, long lines of men waited to buy food and drink, tools, implements, and supplies. He pushed his prices higher, and still the business grew. Shrewd Sam Brannan would make his fortune without wading the icy waters of the American River.

At the sawmill, fifty miles upstream, Jim Marshall saw the gold seekers coming. At first they paid him a small fee to dig in his river property, but soon the fortune hunters overran the whole region. Marshall was swamped. He began gold-hunting for himself, but everywhere he went he found men there before him. All up and down the valley they were digging into the riverbank, the sandbars, and the dry side gulches.

Moody Jim Marshall had liked the solitude of the American River. Now the solitude was gone.

The First Diggings

To FIND a fortune a man needed only a pick, a shovel, and a pan.
With that equipment hundreds hurried into the mountains. At
night the valleys twinkled with campfires, and by day thousands
of picks and shovels hacked at the ledges and dug up the stream
beds. It was a wet, cold job, wading in snow water and working
in canyons where the sun never shone. But every day brought new
prospectors, their eyes burning with gold fever.

The Sierra Nevada, named by the Spanish, meant "snowy mountains." Now they were the mountains of gold. "The whole country," wrote the editor of the California *Star*, "from the seashore to the base of the Sierra Nevada resounds to the sordid cry of Gold! Gold! Gold! The fields are left half-planted, the houses half-built. Everything is neglected but the manufacture of shovels and pickaxes and the means of transportation to Captain Sutter's Valley." Having published that statement, the editor left his office, bought a pick and shovel, and started for the diggings.

At Sutter's Fort a young man named John Bidwell kept the records of John Sutter's business. Bidwell had been a schoolteacher in Ohio before he grew restless and went west. He arrived in California in 1841, in the first wagon train from the Missouri. In California he bought land on the Feather River and went to work for Captain Sutter.

Now, in 1848, seeing the rush of prospectors, John Bidwell grew restless again. He could not stay at his desk with all that excitement around him.

Bidwell knew the country around Coloma where Marshall's

sawmill stood. That American River Valley was much like the Feather River country. Both streams rushed through gulches and canyons and both of them formed sandbars on the flats. Instead of following the herd, Bidwell followed his head. He reasoned that in both valleys the river would wash gold from the mountains; in both valleys the gold would lodge in sandbars and ledges. John Bidwell loaded a packhorse and headed north toward Feather River.

The Feather River joins the Sacramento twenty miles from the site of Sutter's Fort. As soon as he turned up the Feather, Bidwell found specks of gold at the river's edge. The heavier particles, he reasoned, would not be washed so far from the gold deposits in the hills. With high hopes he hurried up the river. He found his first nuggets on a wide sandbar where the river tumbled out of a gorge. This became the rich and famous Bidwell's Bar.

Around Bidwell's Bar a camp sprang up. Men slept in tents, lean-to's, and wagons, or in a blanket on the ground. From daybreak till dark they dug for gold. There were no stores, no shops, no restaurants or hotels. Everyone was a fortune hunter. The men who came in lightly laden could stay only till their bacon and beans were gone. Then they had to go back to Sutter's Fort for more supplies. They met hundreds of others on the way.

By midsummer there were many new diggings. While Bidwell was leading the way up Feather River, other men were finding gold in new places. A French lumberjack, who had quit his job with Captain Sutter, opened rich diggings at Weberville. An American rancher found gold under Mount Shasta. A German settler struck gold along the Mokelumne, and his Indian workmen found rich deposits on the Stanislaus.

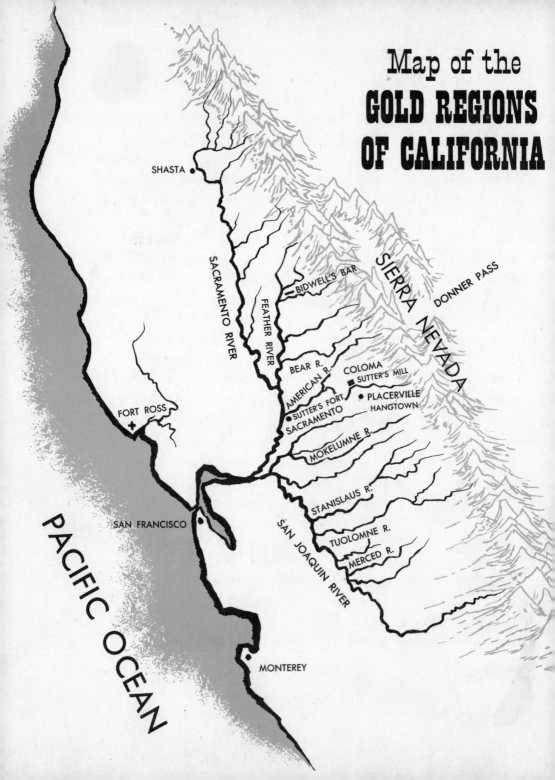

Look on the map and see how the rivers run down from the central Sierras. The Merced, Tuolomne, Stanislaus, and Moke-lumne all flow into the San Joaquin. The Bear and the Feather and the two forks of the American River all join the Sacramento. Each of these streams, tumbling down from the snowy mountains, became a goal of the gold seekers. In each valley mining camps sprang up. If a man had no luck in one digging, he could try another. By the end of the first summer there were five thousand prospectors — "a restless, racing, rummaging, ragged multitude," said a man who watched them scrambling through the mountains.

The first prospectors panned for gold anywhere. They were like a flock of blackbirds in a field, scratching the earth, picking up some morsels, and hurrying on. But as the camps grew and mining became more thorough, the miners established regulations. They agreed that a man should have his own claim, which no one else could "jump" until he gave it up. The claims might be as small as a wagon bed or as large as a barn floor. On sandbars the claims were smaller than on hillsides and in broad valleys. To mark his claim a miner scratched a line around it and stuck his shovel in.

The first prospectors mined for gold with a washpan. Scooping up sand and gravel in a pan of water, they swirled it around so that the sand washed over the rim; the heavier gold settled in the bottom and was picked out from the stones. Soon came the rocker, or cradle. This was a wooden box, with a wire screen bottom, mounted on curved runners. "Dirt" was shoveled into the box. Then the cradle was rocked, and water was poured in. Sand washed through the screen, and the gold remained, to be picked out from the coarse pebbles. Often two or three partners worked a cradle together.

Around the diggings, tents and cabins sprang up and stores appeared. On rough wagon roads, supplies came in, and bags of gold went out. Gold was plentiful in the early diggings. Any man could average $10 worth a day, and a lucky man might turn up a big nugget worth thousands. The men who opened the first stores, restaurants and hotels had gold mines of their own. Goods freighted over the mountain roads brought fantastic prices. Eggs sold for $1.00 each. Beef from worn-out oxen brought $20 a pound. In one remote camp a man sold the shirt off his back for $300.

By the end of 1848, the diggings had yielded $10 million in gold. There were about ten thousand miners in the camps. All were men from the West Coast, from California and Oregon. California was a remote place then. But the next year would bring a rush of fortune seekers from the outside world.

Ho California! That's the Place for Me!

Gold is a small word but a powerful one. It took a long time for news to spread in 1848, but the magic word went to distant places. Everywhere it went it inflamed minds and emotions.

That summer the word reached Honolulu when a San Francisco ship put in. On its return the ship was crammed with gold seekers.

A California man wrote a letter to his brother in Oregon. Settlers there dropped their plows and axes and packed their wagons for Sacramento.

From California an official report of the mines was sent to President Polk in Washington. As there was no traveled route across the mountains, the messenger took a ship from San Francisco to Peru, where he boarded another ship to Panama. After crossing the isthmus, he sailed to the island of Jamaica and there embarked in a trading vessel for New Orleans. His account of California gold sent waves of excitement through the city. After a stagecoach journey to Washington, he delivered his report along with some lumps of gold from the California diggings.

President Polk wanted the American nation to expand across the entire continent. He had just acquired the Far West as a Territory. Now he made a dramatic announcement of the importance of California. In a message to Congress at the end of 1848 he said, "The abundance of gold in California Territory . . . would scarcely command belief." He stated that thousands of men were already finding rich deposits of gold in many different locations.

Newspapers in all the states published this message, often enlarging upon its promise of riches. "The ground is . . . one vast gold mine." "Men have picked up $1,800, $1,500, $1,200 in a single day," reported the papers. Cartoons showed excited men digging up fortunes.

Soon thousands of men were preparing to go to California. "Argonauts" they were called, from the Greek myth of Jason and his companions on the ship *Argo* who went in search of the Golden Fleece.

People in the East had only vague ideas about the Pacific Coast, but suddenly "California" had become a magic name. All through the eastern states men were singing:

> Ho California!
> That's the land for me.
> I'm off for Sacramento
> With my washpan on my knee.

The newspapers gave advice on collecting, melting, and testing gold. Merchants advertised medicines and money belts for men going to California.

But how to get there? The first Argonauts went by ship, like the ancient Jason.

The Best Chance Yet
for
CALIFORNIA!

CALIFORNIA
Emigrants
LOOK HERE!!
the fast sailing ship *Challenge*

FOR
CALIFORNIA!
on the very fast sailing
Barque Emma ISIDORA

These picture posters appeared in town halls and railroad stations, on barn doors and board fences in all the eastern cities.

There were three sea routes to California. Some parties sailed all the way around South America and up the Pacific coast to San Francisco. Others sailed to Panama or to Nicaragua in Central America, where they toiled through the jungle and over the mountains to the Pacific side. Another ship took them to San Francisco.

From the interior states, the way to California was the long overland trail, across prairies, plains, deserts and mountains. For ten years the Oregon Trail had been traveled by emigrants to the Northwest. The Argonauts followed the Oregon Trail as far as the Great Salt Lake in Utah. From there they crossed the great desert to California.

In the central states bordering the Ohio River, hundreds of California companies were formed. These were parties banding together for the overland journey. Impatiently they waited for spring so that their oxen, mules and horses could graze on the western prairie. They took steamboats to "jumping-off" places on the Missouri — Independence, St. Joseph, Council Bluffs. At these points they formed wagon trains for the long trail west.

California had become a magic name even across the Atlantic. The year 1848 was a grim time in Europe. In Ireland a potato famine left thousands dead of starvation, and on the continent there were hunger, revolution, and unemployment. In this dark time, the news of gold in California came like a sunrise. California handbooks and guidebooks appeared in England, France, Holland, and Germany.

The great rush of 1849 would bring people to California from every state in America and every country of Europe. A dozen languages would sound in the saloons of Hangtown and Dutchman's Flat.

FOR
CALIFORNIA
Mutual Protection
Trading & Mining Co.

Voyage of the "West Wind"

For
CALIFORNIA!
Mutual Protection
Trading & Mining Co.
Having purchased the very fast Sailing Ship
WEST WIND
will leave about the 15th of February, 1849. This vessel will
be fitted in the very best manner. Every member pays $300
and is entitled to an equal portion of all the profits made by
the company. Experienced men are engaged as officers of the
company. A rare chance is offered to any wishing to make
Large Profits. The Company is limited to 60. Make immediate
application to
JAMES H. PRICE, Agent
23 State Street, corner of Devonshire St., Boston.

WHILE Calvin Rowe watched these posters rolling out of his
uncle's printing press in north Boston, he began to dream of California. His twenty-first birthday was approaching, and his father
had given him $500 to start a printing business of his own. But
suddenly the printing trade seemed like a prison.

The posters were to be displayed in public places around Boston. Before they left the printing press, they had enlisted a fortune
hunter.

When the *West Wind* scudded out of Boston harbor, Calvin Rowe stood at the rail. He watched the city dwindle and the Boston Lighthouse pass. Then there was only the gray ocean. Around him were the "company," tradesmen, farmers, business men, all with excitement in their eyes. They were leaving staid New England for adventurous California.

Ahead of them was one of the longest voyages in the world — 17,000 miles around Cape Horn and up the long coast of the Pacific. It would take five months if the winds were fair; seven months, more likely. At San Francisco the fortune hunters would sell their ship and go to the mines. They had months to plan the future of their "company."

The sea grew rough, and the *West Wind* pitched and tossed. For a week the seasick Argonauts lost their enthusiasm. When they got their sea legs their spirits revived. One fine morning Calvin Rowe climbed the mainmast to look for passing ships. Below he heard a squealing and grunting. In a pen on the foredeck were twenty pigs. There would be fresh meat on the long voyage.

In the long weeks that followed, the traders memorized maps of California and studied books about gold mining. They read about "placers," "rockers," "flumes" and "sluices" and talked of gold-bearing sands and gold nuggets. After religious services, they sang their favorite song:

> I came from Massachusetts
> With a washbowl on my knee;
> I'm going to California,
> The gold dust for to see.
> It rained all night the day I left,

The weather it was dry;
The sun so hot I froze to death,
Oh, brothers, don't you cry.
Ho California!
That's the place for me.
I'm off to Sacramento
With my washbowl on my knee.

While weeks grew into months, they kept their excitement burning.

Impatiently they traced the ship's progress on the sea charts. Under a blazing sun they crossed the equator. In howling gales of wind they rolled around Cape Horn. When the sky blew clear, they saw the sun setting on their port bow and they knew they had turned northward. Now they were headed straight for California. But it seemed years since they had been on land.

One of the endless discussions in the cabin centered around the

various ways of getting to California. While the *West Wind* was
rounding South America, thousands of Argonauts were on a shorter
journey. From Boston, New York or Baltimore they took a steamer
to Panama. In native canoes they were taken through the swamps
of the Chagres River. On muleback they crossed the mountain
jungle, where parrots screamed and monkeys chattered, to the
Pacific. There a steamer took them north to San Francisco.

On this route many died of cholera and yellow fever. Others had to wait for weeks for steamer passage on the Pacific side. The longer trip around Cape Horn, the "company" agreed, was better than the short cut across Panama.

In the last week of June, after more than twenty weeks at sea, a new excitement filled the *West Wind*. From the masthead Calvin Rowe saw a dark, firm line beyond the water. California, at last! The next morning the whole company was on deck at sunrise. They cheered as the ship sailed through the Golden Gate.

San Francisco, in the year 1849, was a city of tents spreading over the harbor hills. The dusty streets were thronged with miners from the mountains and emigrants heading for the mines. Chinese with long pigtails, Mexican mule drivers, traders, gamblers, prospectors jostled each other in the plaza. In the harbor lay dozens of abandoned ships. The *West Wind* joined them, swinging in the tide on rusted anchor chains.

With no buyer for their ship, the "company" had no funds to invest in mining land and nothing to hold them together. Now it was every man for himself. Some wanted to go to Sacramento, others to Feather River, still others to the Stanislaus. So the "company" separated.

Calvin Rowe said goodbye to his shipmates. He wondered what fortunes they would have and whether they would meet again. Then he started for the diggings at Grizzly Flats, in the hills beyond the Sacramento.

On the Trail

IN THE SPRING of 1849, in Wabash County, Ill., Jim Connor left his father's cornfield for the gold fields of California. He joined a party called the "Wabash Pioneers." They went by stagecoach to St. Louis and there took a steamboat, the *Bald Eagle,* up the Missouri.

The *Bald Eagle* was crowded with wagons, baggage, mules, oxen, and restless gold seekers. Many of them got off at Independence, near present Kansas City, to begin the long trek by trail. The Wabash Pioneers went on to St. Joe, another "jumping-off place" for the Far West.

St. Joe lay on the edge of settlement, but it was full of life and excitement. Hundreds of tents, tepees, carts and wagons were scattered along the riverbank. Over the trampled ground came the clang of blacksmiths' anvils, the creaking of wagon wheels, the bellowing of cattle, and the shrill *hee-haw* of mules.

Here the Wabash Pioneers bought wagons, mules, and oxen. They hired a guide who had been to the Pacific. They filled a chuck wagon with flour, bacon, beans, rice, tea, coffee, sugar, salt, dried apples, lard, and cornmeal.

On their last night, Jim Connor wrote a letter home to Illinois and went to the steamboat landing to mail it. In his letter he had written: "It seems that half of mankind is here, getting ready for the trail." Now he would have said "all mankind." He passed a family gathered around their fire for evening prayer, a circle of men dealing cards on a blanket by lantern light, a mother soothing a sick child, a young fellow strumming a banjo, a ragged, barefoot man racing around holding up two big potatoes and crying, "Gold! Gold!" Truly all kinds of men were here, rich and poor, sober and frenzied, farmers and preachers, the strong and the weak, the old and the young.

At the landing Jim found a river captain talking to an army officer, with a circle of men around them.

"They are waiting now on the levee in St. Louis," the riverman said. "Thousands of them, and more coming every day."

"There will be 50,000 on the trail this summer," the army officer said. "Enough to make a state out of California — if they all get there."

"They won't all get there," said a weathered wagonmaster.

"There's big mountains, I hear," said a tired-looking man at the edge of the circle.

The wagonmaster took a pinch of tobacco from his pouch. "It's not the high mountains or the big rivers or the thieving Indians that turn them back. It's the everyday traveling with no let-up for fever, cholera, rain, hail, dust storms, prairie fires, or broken wagon wheels. It's those miles to cover every day."

"How many miles?" a man asked.

"You figure it," said the wagonmaster. "We've got four months from the time the grass turns green till the snows pile up in the Sierras. Four months and 2,100 miles."

"Figures near twenty miles a day," someone said.

"Every day," said the wagonmaster.

Jim posted his letter and walked on. Soon he heard a hoarse voice and saw a crowd gathered on the riverbank. Standing on a wagon bed, a gaunt, long-bearded man was holding up a lantern and a Bible. It was Sunday, Jim realized, and here was a preacher shouting about Moses and the Promised Land.

Jim went on, past the outlying camps, to a grassy hilltop under the quiet stars. Behind him lay the twinkling fires of the emigrants and the great dark bend of the river. Westward stretched the vast dark plain. The grass was green now, and the wagons could roll. Tomorrow the Wabash Pioneers would be on the way.

Next morning, the first day of May, they loaded the final provisions and supplies. With a crack of whips the train pulled out. Jim Connor drove the chuck wagon at the end of the line. From the high, swaying seat he saw the trampled trail stretching ahead over the grassy swells of prairie. The sky arched blue, the wind was fresh and free. As they rolled westward, Jim sang:

> There's plenty of gold,
> So I've been told,
> On the banks of the Sacramento.

This was better than plowing his father's cornfield in Wabash County.

A month later he was not so sure. Halfway across a prairie swale, the wagon settled in the mud. The mules, sunk to their bellies, had to be unharnessed. The wagon had to be unloaded. Knee deep in mud and water, Jim carried boxes and barrels to higher ground. They pried up the wagon. Shoving and hauling, they inched it through the mud. They made camp at midnight in a pelting rain. **1177396**

Two months later Jim Connor was brown as an Indian. From the rocky floor of a canyon, his sun-narrowed eyes lifted to towering cliffs. The Devil's Gate. Somehow they had to climb the road that zigzagged upward. *"Gee-up! Gee-up!"* cried the teamsters. The mules leaned into their collars and the iron-rimmed wagon wheels clashed on the stones. Above the Devil's Gate shimmered distant summits, white with snow.

Three months later, in the valley of the Humboldt, the mules floundered through burning sand. Along the trail lay dead horses, mules and oxen, and broken wagons. To lighten their loads, travelers had discarded precious belongings. Through dust-reddened eyes, Jim saw boots, clothing, beds, stoves, cooking implements, harness, and horseshoes. Among these cast-off things stood crude crosses scratched with the names of men who had not made it to California. Up ahead a teamster began singing in a ragged voice. Jim licked his cracked lips and joined in:

> I'll scrape the mountains clean, my boys,
> I'll drink the rivers dry,
> I'll fill my pockets full of rocks,
> So brothers, don't you cry.

On the tenth of September they toiled over the crest of the Sierras and began the steep descent. Three days later, excited as schoolboys, they rolled in to Hangtown. (Here had occurred the first executions for murder in the gold mines.) Scattered over a stumpy clearing were tents and shanties. Men were digging in the ravine and building wooden flumes, or channels, to divert river water.

Here the Wabash Pioneers made their last camp. From the Hangtown miners they learned about new diggings in the valley. The next day they went on to Sutter's Fort.

Many nights, under the desert stars, the Wabash Pioneers had talked of making a mining camp of their own. But now that the journey was over, they scattered, each man for himself. Jim Connor was headed for Grizzly Flats. He had heard that men were finding riches there.

Life at Grizzly Flats

ANGEL'S CAMP, Dogtown, Chinese Ferry, Bullfrog Gulch, You Bet, Yankee Hill, Mule Creek, Christmas Bar, Groundhog Glory, Shirttail Canyon, Tuttletown, Emigrant's Gap — these were the first settlements in the steep Sierra valleys. On the riverbank men hacked at the ledges, shoveled up sand and gravel, carried water to their clumsy rockers. At each place many were toiling for a few dollars a day while a few lucky ones were finding fortunes.

One camp was as flimsy and alluring as another, but Jim Connor went on to Grizzly Flats. He liked the name. It sounded like danger and promise.

The road to Grizzly Flats climbed over Bear Mountain and dropped down to a shelf of land along the river. Over the road came men on foot, on muleback and horseback, and a few in carts and wagons. Some men came emptyhanded, but Jim had a blanket roll on one shoulder and a shovel on the other.

He found a huddle of tents and shanties under the mountainside. In the center of town were a few stores and a hotel run by two Chinese with long pigtails hanging down their backs. A bed cost $10 a night, so Jim decided to camp out. In the crowded restaurant eggs cost $1.00 each, hash $1.50, fried chicken $3.00. Jim left, still hungry. At a store he bought a frying pan, some bacon, beans, and dried apples. He cooked his supper under a pine tree and rolled up in his blanket.

After a week of prospecting, Jim Connor had two ounces of gold. He had marked out a claim in a side canyon two miles up the valley. On Sunday he went in to Grizzly Flats to sell his gold, get supplies and hear the news.

There was no church in Grizzly Flats, but a bell rang every hour. Each time the bell rang, a crowd pressed through a gate in a high board fence. It cost a dollar to get in.

"What's the attraction?" Jim asked a man beside him.

"Cock fight," the stranger said. "Best show in town."

Jim paid his dollar and entered a cockpit enclosed by a circle of board seats. On a bare circle of ground two roosters flew at each other, hissing and striking with their spurs. Some of the spectators shouted for "Warrior." Others cheered for "Little Red."

"Want to make a bet?" asked a man in a derby hat and a red vest.

Jim shook his head.

38

"Piker," the man muttered. He turned to a youth sitting beside Jim. "Here's a sporting man. New shirt and new boots. Want to wager, my friend? Take your choice of the roosters."

"No thanks," the youth said.

"I'll bet gold dust," said the man, holding up a leather pouch. "I'll take Little Red and give you two ounces to an ounce of yours."

"I haven't any gold dust," the youth said. "I just got here."

"From where, friend?"

"From Boston."

"Yankee," the man muttered. "I'm wasting my time."

When the cock fight was over, with Little Red victorious, Jim Connor walked out with the youth from Boston.

"You're new here," Jim said.

"Yes. I just arrived. I came with a company but it broke up in San Francisco."

Jim smiled. "Like me. I came with the Wabash Pioneers. But they're all scattered now."

"My name is Calvin Rowe," said the newcomer.

"I'm Jim Connor, from Wabash County, Ill. I've staked a claim up in Grizzly Gulch." Suddenly he said, "Let's go partners."

Calvin Rowe put out his hand. "I'd like to."

The two partners spent a week building a shack in the gulch. Then they worked the claim together. At first they used a rocker, shoveling "dirt" into the box and washing it through with endless pails of water. Some days they found only a few flakes of gold; other days yielded an ounce of gold dust and small nuggets. An ounce of gold was worth about $15.

Later in the season they built a "long tom" — a wooden trough twelve feet long and a foot wide. The lower end was slotted with

40

crossbars to make a coarse sieve. They dragged the long tom to the edge of the creek and let a stream of water into it. Beneath the sieve was a cleated box to catch the particles of gold. One of the partners shoveled "dirt" into the tom, while the other cleared away the "tailings" of sand and rock. The long tom enabled them to wash more earth with less labor.

All winter they worked the claim. At evening, watching the stars come over Bear Mountain, they talked about the fortunes they had heard of. A man down the river had found a vein of gold that yielded thousands of dollars. Two partners on Coyote Hill had dug up a nugget as big as an orange. A Mexican had come into the Flats with two saddlebags bulging with gold dust.

But already mining was changing. Now half the men in Grizzly Flats were laborers, working for mining companies. They guided the river into a wooden sluice; then they mined the dry riverbed. They hacked out cliffs of quartz and carried the ore to crushing mills. The old individual placer mining was ending.

Jim Connor and Calvin Rowe had no desire to work for wages under the direction of a mining engineer. But their claim was running out. Some days their long tom did not yield a trace of gold. On the best days they found only a few yellow grains.

Spring brought a restlessness to the two partners. Some of their gold had been used to buy provisions in Grizzly Flats. The rest was in a leather pouch under a board in the shanty floor. The pouch weighed about three pounds. That would be nearly $800 worth of gold.

In Grizzly Flats gold brought $14 an ounce, but in San Francisco it brought $16. On a bright May morning the partners threw their packs on their shoulders and started down the trail. They were going to sell their gold in San Francisco.

City of the Golden Gate

THE *Niantic* was originally a sailing ship from New York. Now it was a two-story hotel on the San Francisco waterfront. Here the two young partners slept on the floor. After camping in the mountains, the bare floor was a comfortable bed.

They woke at daylight to the clatter of hammers. Hundreds of buildings were rising among the tents and lean-to's on the harbor hills. A hazy sunrise warmed the coastal mountains across the bay. Quickly the city came to life. Tent flaps were thrown back,

doors swung open in the shops and stores. Out in the harbor small boats pulled from ship to ship. Carts and wagons began loading on the waterfront. It was a cool, clear morning with a fresh breeze blowing through the Golden Gate.

As the two miners walked up the street, bells were ringing for breakfast. Hotels, restaurants and open-sided lunchrooms all had bells to attract customers. At stalls along the harborfront, Chinese vendors sold doughnuts, coffee cake, and cinnamon rolls. The two miners ate avidly. After months of bacon and beans, they gorged on the fresh-baked pastries.

Then they walked up Montgomery Street. Mexicans in big sombreros, men from Chile and Peru in long brown ponchos, Chinese in colored gowns and tassel caps, foreign sailors in blue and white uniforms, Americans from Texas, Virginia, Ohio, and New England — all jostled together in this street of all nations. Among the

44

crowd passed miners, like these two from Grizzly Flats. They were easy to distinguish with their red shirts, battered boots, and faces brown as leather.

Drifting with the crowd, the two partners came to the busy plaza. On plank benches and at refreshment stands, men were conducting business in various languages. Along one side of the plaza ran the big, canvas-covered Eldorado. It looked like a circus tent, and it had a sawdust floor. Inside were clubrooms, land agents, and shipping, express and stagecoach offices. There were also gambling rooms and a gold exchange.

Jim Connor and Calvin Rowe watched the assayer test and weigh their gold. Then he counted out money. When they left the exchange, they had nearly $400 each tied up in their buckskin pouches.

"Game of monte, young sirs?" said an English gambler. He had a curled mustache and wore striped trousers and a checked vest. "See you're in from the mountains."

They shook their heads and went outside. While they were crossing the plaza, the crowd scattered in all directions. Carpenters leaped behind piles of planks. Peddlers hurried their pushcarts around the corners.

Through the plaza raced a bull with horns as wide as a wagon. Behind the animal came two Mexican cowboys. Shouting and swinging their lariats, they pounded after the bull. A lariat snaked through the air and settled over the bull's horns. The horse stopped, and the cowboy looped his lariat around the saddlehorn. At the end of the taut line, the bull sprawled in the dust. When the dazed animal got up, the second cowboy had a rope around him. Docile now, as meek as a mule, the bull was led off to the slaughterhouse.

Jim Connor's eyes were shining. "Did you see those horses? The first one had a blaze on his head like my herding pony back home."

Calvin Rowe was buying a California *Star* from a news vendor. "Look here!" he said. "The first newspaper I've seen since I left Boston."

Quickly the plaza filled again. At noon bells and gongs began a dinner clangor. The partners walked down Kearney Street to a two-story building on a corner. The lower floor was a market. Walls were hung with quarters of beef and mutton and the floor was piled with potatoes, turnips and Sandwich Island squashes. Under a sign $2.00 EACH stood a mound of cabbages on a counter. Those cabbages had been shipped 17,000 miles to California.

The upper floor was a restaurant with two rows of long tables already nearly filled. The partners took the last seats and feasted on salmon trout and venison.

In the afternoon a fog rolled in from the bay, but the clamor and clatter of the city went on. Later the sun broke through and the mist scattered. Down Montgomery Street came a shrilling of fifes and a rattle of drums. The crowd parted as four horses passed. They were drawing a cage-wagon containing a huge grizzly bear. On the wagon a colored placard announced:

Golden Gate Arena
GREAT ATTRACTION!
Two Bulls and One Bear

It was the favorite amusement of San Francisco — the fighting of bears and bulls.

47

A gust of wind swept down the hill. It brought a cloud of golden dust and another bank of fog. The crowd moved on, and the two partners lost each other. They did not meet again till nightfall, in front of the *Niantic* hotel.

Jim Connor stood looking up at the glimmering city. With lamps and lanterns burning, all the canvas dwellings glowed with light. Torches flared from the gambling houses and the night wind brought music from the dance halls.

Calvin Rowe found his partner there.

"I lost you," he said. "Did you go to the bull-and-bear fight?"

"No," said Jim. "Did you?"

Calvin shook his head. He pulled a newspaper from his pocket. "I went to the office of the California *Star*. I got a job there, in the printing room. I start work tomorrow."

"That's good," Jim said. "I start tomorrow, too."

"Where?"

"On a ranch down the valley. I've got money enough to buy a good horse and an outfit."

For a moment they were silent, thinking of their claim in Grizzly Gulch.

"No more rocking the cradle," said Jim, "or feeding the long tom."

"We didn't find a fortune," said his partner. "But we got our share."

New Diggings

THE TWO longest rivers in California are the San Joaquin and the Sacramento. They begin four hundred miles apart, but they end in the same place — in San Francisco Bay. The Sacramento runs south, and the San Joaquin runs north. Both are fed by westward-flowing rivers pouring down from the Sierras. Each of their tributaries had a gold rush in the 1850s.

Miners soon overran the foothill country. They worked up the rivers in search of gold-bearing bars and ledges. They made lonely camps in remote places. Wherever they found gold, they stayed. Other miners came, a camp grew up, a new town was started. No place was too distant or difficult for prospectors in search of gold.

Down from the hills came news of new discoveries. One excitement followed another, each one reported to be "the richest yet." Some of their discoveries never "panned out."

In 1855 there was excited talk of gold on the Kern River, and the San Francisco papers reported rich deposits there. The Kern River lay far south of the mining district, in an unexplored region. Five thousand men rushed into that wild country. A few prospectors found traces of gold in the Kern River, most of them found nothing. In disgust they named their town Humbug.

Another false report lured men to Meadow Lake, high in the mountains. Three thousand miners swarmed in, and 150 buildings were erected at timber line. Hundreds of claim notices were scratched on the rocky hillside. After a bitter winter and no rich discoveries, men began to drift away. Three years later the "city" of Meadow Lake was lifeless.

Another windswept camp was Bodie, in high country near the California-Nevada border. It failed and was deserted, like Meadow Lake. Ten years later a wandering prospector found a rich chamber of ore at the edge of this ghost town. A second rush to Bodie made it one of the busiest mining towns in the West. To follow the veins of gold, miners dug into the streets and under buildings. Fortunes were made on claims that had been abandoned a few years before.

For ten years emigrant wagon trains had toiled over a mountain on the Nevada-California border. They had lurched over ledges of blue rock, hurrying on to the gold camps. In 1859 it was discovered that the blue rock was rich in silver.

In the early 1860s thousands of miners rushed to this new "Silverado." Hundreds of them made fortunes from the silver

ledges. But the veins of ore led deep underground, beyond the reach of pick and shovel. The great wealth of the silver mines was developed by mining companies. They opened deep shafts and sent hundreds of Chinese miners to work far underground. In the famous silver town of Virginia City, blasts of dynamite shook the streets. Inside the mountain were miles of shafts and tunnels.

After ten years the California mines were declining. Some prospectors returned to the East. Others took up ranching and farming. Many went on looking for gold in other places. They started new diggings all the way from Arizona to Montana and Idaho.

In 1862 some ragged prospectors came in to the town of Bannock, Mont. They bought supplies, saying nothing about the gold nuggets they used for pay. When they left, nearly all the citizens of Bannock followed them to their diggings on Grasshopper Creek. Next year found ten thousand men, nearly the whole white population of Montana, scratching for gold in Alder Canyon and Last Chance Gulch. Some of the lucky ones invested their profits in big Montana cattle ranches.

In 1858 a party of thirty discouraged men were camped on the site of Denver, Colo. They had been prospecting without success, and now they were giving up. But one of them, a miner from California, kept on looking. After the rest had gone he found a pocket of gold at the foot of the mountains. At the same time another prospector was finding gold seventy miles south, in the shadow of Pike's Peak.

This news brought new caravans of fortune hunters. A hundred thousand wagons painted PIKE'S PEAK OR BUST! creaked across Nebraska in 1859. For many of the "Fifty-niners," the rush to Colorado ended in disappointment. Thousands turned back, crossing the plains with their wagons labeled BUSTED, BY GOSH!

But there were riches buried in the Colorado hills. Mining companies tunneled into mountainsides and built stamp mills to crush the ore and free the precious metals. For fifty years the Colorado mines produced large yields of gold, silver, copper and lead.

Ghost Towns and Busy Cities

IN A FEW YEARS the Gold Rush peopled the western mountains. It brought civilization to remote places that might have remained wilderness for years to come. In 1848 the border of settlement was the Missouri River, barely halfway across the continent. Clusters of habitation were beginning in Oregon and Utah, but these settlements were almost lost in the empty spaces of the Far West. The Gold Rush carried the American nation across the continent. It made the United States a coast-to-coast country.

Mining always comes to an end. It is a process of depletion, a taking out of what nature has stored in the earth. The gold mines became exhausted, and the miners moved on. But the Gold Rush had created new states which continued to grow and develop. After the gold was gone, people discovered less dramatic but more lasting riches in the West. They developed the great farming

valleys of California, the big cattle ranches of Montana, the Rocky Mountain resources of timber and waterpower.

Some of the flimsy gold camps grew into busy commercial cities. Sutter's Fort became Sacramento, Hangtown became Placerville. Last Chance Gulch in Montana became the capital city of Helena. The gold camp of Aurora became Denver, the metropolis of Colorado.

But hundreds of mining camps in remote places were left deserted after the gold was gone. They can be seen today in the western mountains. Towns once full of excitement are now silent and lifeless. The roofs have sagged with winter snows. Doors hang on rusty hinges. Fences and walls are broken, tumbleweed grows in the streets, gophers nest under a faded LODGING HOUSE sign. Only the tracks of wolves and coyotes are printed in the snow.

Many of the ghost towns are on old roads that few people travel now. Some can be reached only by a rocky trail. Some are in deep canyons, some on windswept slopes at timberline. But all have their memories of restless men and dreams of riches.

Old stories and legends hang over the ghost towns. A man looking for a lost mule in a lonely canyon stumbled upon a chunk of gold as big as a pumpkin. A boy picking up stones for his slingshot found a nugget worth a thousand dollars. A farmer found some pockets of earth rooted up by his hogs and then washed by the winter rains; from one pocket he took $5,000 in gold, and from another $8,000. Two discouraged partners gave up their claim, leaving a shovel stuck in a sand bank. Along came a prospector who turned up the shovel and saw a glint of yellow. He took $40,000 out of the abandoned claim.

Now the voice of the ghost towns is the sough and sigh of the mountain winds. Nothing is left but memories. There are memories of success and memories of failure.

The two men with whom the Gold Rush began were John A. Sutter and James W. Marshall. For them the treasure of the Sierras brought ruin. Sutter's lands were overrun by gold-crazed miners. His workmen left their shops and fields, his horses were stolen, his sheep and cattle slaughtered. In 1852, the year of California's greatest gold production, Sutter was bankrupt. For a while the state of California gave him a pension. When that stopped, he went to Washington, D.C., to claim his lost lands in California. He died there, penniless, while waiting for justice.

To James Marshall the Gold Rush brought nothing but misfortune. The bit of gold he found in the millrace that historic morning in 1848 was worth about fifty cents. It led to great fortunes for other men, but Marshall never made a lucky strike. He

wandered around the mining camps, always too late to stake a rich claim. He made a scanty living by selling autographs on a printed card that showed a picture of the old Sutter Mill. The card read:

autograph of
Jas. W. Marshall
The Discoverer of Gold in California
January, 1848

In 1872 the state of California granted Marshall a small pension. In his last years he worked as a gardener at Coloma, the site of the old Sutter Mill. His cabin is preserved there. Beside it stands a memorial bronze figure of the man who discovered gold but died in poverty.

Index

6382